Leadership in Crisis:

Navigating Toxic Employees in Public Service

By: Jeremey Criner

"This book is your go-to playbook for turning toxic chaos into a thriving, respectful workplace, providing practical tools and strategies to lead with confidence and integrity in the public sector.

With over 20 years in the public sector environment, I can say without question that the number one complaint from leaders is dealing with toxic employees and the issues that come along with them."

Contents

Introduction 2

Chapter 1: Understanding Toxicity in the Workplace 5

Chapter 2: Common Types of Toxic Behaviors 9

Chapter 3: Creating a Healthy Work Environment 13

Chapter 4: Early Detection and Reporting Mechanisms ... 19

Chapter 5: Addressing Toxic Behaviors 25

Chapter 6: Legal and Ethical Considerations 31

Chapter 7: Remedial Actions and Outcomes 37

Chapter 8: Case Studies and Practical Examples 44

Conclusion: The Road to a Thriving Workplace 51

Further Resources 55

Introduction

Welcome to the wild world of public employment! Whether you're a seasoned HR professional, a fresh-faced manager, or simply someone curious about workplace dynamics, you've come to the right place. Dealing with toxic employees is like navigating a minefield—one wrong step, and boom! But don't worry; we've got your back. This book is your trusty guide to handling those tricky situations with grace, empathy, and a dash of humor.

Why This Book?

You might be wondering, "Why a whole book on toxic employees? Can't we just fire them and move on?" If only it were that simple! In public employment, things aren't always black and white. We're dealing with public trust, taxpayer dollars, and a host of rules and regulations. It's a delicate dance, and sometimes it feels like you're doing the cha-cha on a tightrope. One wrong move, and you could end up in a heap of trouble—or worse, on the front page of the local newspaper.

Quote: "Culture eats strategy for breakfast." - **Peter Drucker**, management guru

Toxic employees aren't just a nuisance; they can be a real threat to your organization's culture and productivity. They drain the energy, spread negativity, and sometimes cause real harm. But here's the good news: You can handle it. With the right tools and mindset, you can turn a toxic situation into an opportunity for growth and improvement.

What You'll Learn

In this book, we're going to break down everything you need to know about dealing with toxic employees in the public sector. We'll start by understanding what makes someone "toxic" and how to spot the warning signs early. Then, we'll dive into practical strategies for managing these tricky individuals—whether they're passive-aggressive saboteurs, chronic complainers, or overly assertive managers. We'll also cover the legal and ethical aspects, because let's face it, the public sector has its own unique set of challenges.

And don't worry, it's not all doom and gloom. We've packed this book with real-life case studies, practical examples, and plenty of tips to help you not just survive but thrive. You'll get to see how others have navigated these choppy waters and come out stronger on the other side.

Quote: "The culture of any organization is shaped by the worst behavior the leader is willing to tolerate." - **Gruenter and Whitaker**, organizational consultants

Why It Matters

You might think, "Is it really worth all this effort? Can't we just ignore the problem?" Well, imagine this: You're working on a crucial project that's set to improve community services. Everything's going great, but then, BAM! A toxic employee starts spreading rumors, undermining colleagues, and throwing the whole team off track. Suddenly, what should have been a smooth ride turns into a bumpy rollercoaster.

In the public sector, where the stakes are high and the spotlight is always on, you can't afford to let things slide. The way you handle toxic employees can make or break your team's morale, your project's success, and even your organization's reputation. So yes, it's worth it.

A Journey Together

Think of this book as a roadmap, a trusty companion on your journey to creating a healthy, vibrant work environment. We're not here to just give you a list of dos and don'ts; we're here to explore, understand, and tackle the root causes of toxic behavior. We're going to laugh a little, learn a lot, and hopefully, make your workplace a better place for everyone.

So, grab a cup of coffee, get comfy, and let's dive in. Together, we'll explore the ins and outs of handling toxic employees in public employment. It's a wild ride, but with the right knowledge and tools, you'll not only navigate the chaos—you'll lead your team to a brighter, healthier workplace.

Let's get started!

Chapter 1: Understanding Toxicity in the Workplace

Welcome! So, you're here because you're dealing with a bit of a tricky situation at work, huh? Or maybe you're just trying to be proactive—smart move! Toxic employees can really throw a wrench into the gears of any workplace, especially in the public sector, where everything needs to run like a well-oiled machine. Let's dive into understanding what makes a workplace toxic and why it's so important to nip these issues in the bud.

Defining Toxic Behavior

First things first, what do we mean by "toxic behavior"? Picture this: You have a colleague who constantly gossips, another who's always negative, and one who's downright aggressive. Sound familiar? These are just a few examples of toxic behavior. In essence, toxic behavior refers to actions and attitudes that poison the work environment and negatively impact others.

But it's not just about bad moods or occasional outbursts. We're talking about persistent, harmful behavior that creates an atmosphere of fear, mistrust, and resentment. It's like having a bad apple that spoils the whole bunch.

Quote: "Culture is not just one aspect of the game, it is the game." - **Lou Gerstner**, former CEO of IBM

The Spectrum of Toxicity: From Mild to Severe

Not all toxic behaviors are created equal. Some are mild annoyances, while others can bring the whole workplace crashing down. Let's break it down:

1. **Mild Toxicity:** This includes behaviors that are irritating but not deeply harmful—think minor gossip or occasional grumbling. While these may

seem harmless, they can add up over time, slowly chipping away at team morale.

2. **Moderate Toxicity:** Now we're getting into more problematic territory. This might be a colleague who is consistently negative, passive-aggressive, or regularly shirks responsibilities. These behaviors start to disrupt workflow and create tension.

3. **Severe Toxicity:** Here's where things get serious. Severe toxicity includes bullying, harassment, sabotage, and other hostile actions. These behaviors create a toxic environment that can lead to high turnover, legal issues, and a damaged organizational reputation.

Quote: "A toxic culture can destroy good people." - **Tony Hsieh**, former CEO of Zappos

Impact on Employee Well-being and Organizational Health

Okay, so now we know what toxic behavior looks like. But why is it such a big deal? The impact of a toxic employee can ripple through the entire organization, causing all sorts of problems.

Employee Well-being

Let's start with the most important part—people. Toxic behavior can take a heavy toll on employees' mental and emotional well-being. Imagine coming to work every day feeling stressed, anxious, or even scared. It's not just unpleasant; it's unhealthy. Employees who are constantly exposed to toxicity may suffer from burnout, depression, and a host of other issues that affect their productivity and overall happiness.

Organizational Health

And it's not just the employees who suffer—the organization takes a hit too. Toxic behavior can lead to decreased productivity, as employees are more focused on dealing with the drama than doing their jobs. Projects get delayed, mistakes happen, and the overall quality of work goes down. In the public sector, where the stakes are high and the spotlight is bright, this can be particularly damaging.

Plus, a toxic environment can tarnish the organization's reputation, making it harder to attract and retain top talent. No one wants to work for—or with—an organization known for its toxic culture.

Quote: "You have to look at the overall company culture. If you've got good people, then they'll lift everyone up." - **Sheryl Sandberg**, COO of Facebook

Conclusion

Understanding what toxic behavior is and recognizing its impact is the first step toward creating a healthier, happier workplace. Remember, a single toxic employee can have a far-reaching effect, but with the right strategies, you can turn things around.

In the upcoming chapters, we'll dive into specific types of toxic behaviors, how to prevent them, and what to do when you encounter them. You'll get practical tips, real-world examples, and expert advice to help you navigate these tricky waters.

So, take a deep breath and let's get ready to tackle toxicity head-on. You've got this!

Quote: "Management is about human beings. Its task is to make people capable of joint performance, to make their strengths effective and their weaknesses irrelevant." - **Peter Drucker**, management consultant and author

Stay tuned for Chapter 2, where we'll start by looking at the common types of toxic behaviors you might encounter and how to spot them early. Let's get to work!

Chapter 2: Common Types of Toxic Behaviors

Welcome to the nitty-gritty! Now that we've dipped our toes into the murky waters of workplace toxicity, it's time to wade in a little deeper. Think of this chapter as your guide to the "greatest hits" of toxic behaviors—though, let's be real, no one's putting these on their playlist. From the snarky saboteur to the chronic complainer, we're about to introduce you to the characters that make the workplace a little less wonderful. But don't worry, we're not just identifying the problem; we're setting the stage for solutions.

The Bully: Intimidation and Harassment

Ah, the classic office bully. We've all seen one at some point—the person who uses fear and intimidation to get their way. This isn't just about playground tactics like name-calling or physical threats (though those are definitely included). Office bullies might use their position or seniority to push others around, belittle their colleagues, or even steal credit for work that isn't theirs.

Impact: Bullies can create a hostile work environment where employees feel unsafe and undervalued. It's not just about hurt feelings—bullying can lead to increased absenteeism, high turnover rates, and even legal issues.

What to Watch For: Frequent interruptions during meetings, public criticism, or an overall aggressive demeanor.

Quote: "In the end, it's not about who is right or wrong, but about finding a solution." - **Simon Sinek**, author and motivational speaker

The Gossip: Spreading Rumors and Creating Divisions

Next up, we have the Gossip. You know the type—the one who always has the latest dirt on everyone and isn't shy about sharing it. While a little bit of water cooler chat can be harmless, gossip becomes toxic when it spreads false information, undermines colleagues, and creates cliques. The Gossip thrives on drama and loves to stir the pot, often making mountains out of molehills.

Impact: Gossip can erode trust and destroy team cohesion. It can lead to an "us vs. them" mentality, making collaboration difficult and creating a culture of suspicion. Plus, once rumors start, they're hard to quash, even if they're totally unfounded.

What to Watch For: Frequent side conversations, whispering, and employees suddenly getting cold shoulders from their peers.

Quote: "A toxic culture can destroy good people." - **Tony Hsieh**, former CEO of Zappos

The Saboteur: Undermining Colleagues and Projects

Enter the Saboteur, the master of covert operations. This person isn't just a critic—they actively work to undermine their colleagues or projects. Whether it's withholding information, setting others up for failure, or spreading misinformation, the Saboteur's goal is to make others look bad while keeping their own hands clean. They're like the stealth bomber of the office—striking quietly and often without warning.

Impact: Sabotage can be devastating, causing projects to fail and careers to derail. It not only affects the targeted individual but can also bring down entire teams. The damage can be costly, both in terms of lost productivity and morale.

What to Watch For: Missing or incomplete information, inexplicable project delays, and a general air of secrecy or confusion.

Quote: "Culture eats strategy for breakfast." - **Peter Drucker**, management guru

The Chronic Complainer: Constant Negativity

Meet the Chronic Complainer. This person never met a situation they couldn't gripe about. Whether it's the workload, the office temperature, or the quality of the free coffee, nothing is ever good enough. While constructive criticism is always welcome, the Chronic Complainer isn't interested in solutions. They're all about the problem, all the time.

Impact: Chronic complaining is a morale killer. It spreads negativity and can make the workplace feel like a giant black hole of despair. Over time, it can sap the energy of even the most enthusiastic employees, leading to a toxic work culture where negativity becomes the norm.

What to Watch For: Constant criticism, a negative tone, and an unwillingness to engage in solution-focused discussions.

Quote: "The true test of a company's culture is how well it treats its people when times are tough." - **Howard Schultz**, former CEO of Starbucks

The Underperformer: Consistent Underachievement

Last but not least, we have the Underperformer. This is the person who just can't seem to meet expectations, no matter how low the bar is set. They might be unmotivated, lack the necessary skills, or simply not care. Whatever the reason, their constant underachievement drags the whole team down.

Impact: Underperformance can lead to missed deadlines, increased workload for other team members, and a general sense of frustration. It's not just about the quality of work—it's about fairness. When one person isn't pulling their weight, it can cause resentment and disrupt team dynamics.

What to Watch For: Missed deadlines, poor-quality work, and frequent excuses.

Quote: "The way to achieve your own success is to be willing to help somebody else get it first." - **Iyanla Vanzant**, inspirational speaker and author

Conclusion

And there you have it—the rogues' gallery of toxic workplace behaviors. From the blustery bully to the grumbling complainer, these characters can turn even the best workplaces into a nightmare. But identifying these behaviors is just the first step. The real challenge is figuring out how to handle them in a way that's fair, effective, and aligned with your organization's values.

In the next chapter, we'll start exploring how to create a healthy work environment that prevents these toxic behaviors from taking root in the first place. We'll cover everything from setting clear expectations to fostering a culture of respect and inclusion. So stick with us—this rollercoaster ride is just getting started!

Until then, keep your eyes open and your team spirit high. You're well on your way to becoming a workplace superhero, ready to tackle any toxic behavior that comes your way. Let's do this!

Chapter 3: Creating a Healthy Work Environment

Alright, team! Now that we've taken a deep dive into the murky waters of toxic behaviors, let's shift gears and focus on the good stuff. Imagine a workplace where everyone feels valued, respected, and motivated. Sounds like a dream, right? But it doesn't have to be. Creating a healthy work environment isn't about waving a magic wand; it's about setting the stage for positive interactions, clear expectations, and a supportive culture. In this chapter, we'll explore practical ways to cultivate a workplace where toxicity doesn't stand a chance.

Establishing Clear Expectations and Policies

Let's start with the basics: setting clear expectations. Think of this as the blueprint for your workplace. Without it, people are left guessing what's acceptable and what's not. Spoiler alert: chaos usually follows. So, how do we lay down the law without being, well, too law-like?

Defining Expectations

First up, spell out what you expect from everyone. This includes professional conduct, communication standards, and even little things like dress code. Be as specific as possible. Vague guidelines like "act professionally" can be interpreted in a million different ways. Instead, say something like, "We expect all employees to communicate respectfully, listen actively, and provide constructive feedback."

This isn't about micromanaging; it's about giving everyone a clear understanding of what's expected. Remember, clarity is kindness. When people know the rules, they can play the game better.

Quote: "The culture of any organization is shaped by the worst behavior the leader is willing to tolerate." - **Gruenter and Whitaker**, organizational consultants

Developing and Communicating Policies

Next, let's talk policies. Yes, we know policies can sound boring, but they're the backbone of a fair and transparent workplace. Your code of conduct, anti-harassment policy, and grievance procedures aren't just documents collecting dust—they're living, breathing guides that help everyone navigate the work environment.

How to Do It Right:

- **Make Them Accessible:** Ensure every employee has easy access to these policies. Whether it's a handbook, an intranet page, or a poster in the break room, make sure it's easy to find.

- **Regular Refreshers:** Don't just hand out these policies once and forget about them. Regularly remind everyone about them, perhaps during onboarding or annual training sessions.

- **Lead by Example:** Managers and leaders, this one's for you. Set the standard by following these policies to the letter. If leadership doesn't walk the talk, why should anyone else?

Promoting Inclusivity and Diversity

Now, let's get to one of the hottest topics in workplace culture: inclusivity and diversity. This isn't just a checkbox on an HR form; it's about creating a space where everyone, regardless of background, feels like they belong. An inclusive workplace isn't just morally right; it's also a powerhouse for innovation and creativity.

Embracing Diversity

Diversity goes beyond race and gender. It includes age, cultural background, sexual orientation, disability, and more. The beauty of diversity is that it brings a wealth of perspectives and experiences to the table. But how do we embrace it?

- **Inclusive Hiring Practices:** Start with the hiring process. Ensure your job postings are inclusive and avoid jargon that might deter non-traditional candidates. Use diverse interview panels and question sets to prevent unconscious bias.
- **Celebrating Differences:** Acknowledge and celebrate the diverse backgrounds of your team members. This could be as simple as celebrating cultural holidays or as involved as hosting diversity workshops.

Quote: "The way to achieve your own success is to be willing to help somebody else get it first." - **Iyanla Vanzant**, inspirational speaker and author

Fostering Inclusivity

Creating an inclusive workplace is about more than just bringing diverse people together. It's about ensuring everyone feels valued and heard. How do we do that?

- **Safe Spaces:** Create forums or groups where employees can share their experiences and feel supported. Employee Resource Groups (ERGs) can be a great way to build community and foster inclusivity.
- **Inclusive Language:** Language matters. Encourage the use of inclusive language that respects all identities. This includes using correct pronouns and avoiding assumptions about people's backgrounds or experiences.

- **Equal Opportunities:** Ensure that everyone has equal access to opportunities, whether it's for professional development, leadership roles, or new projects.

Encouraging Open Communication and Feedback

A healthy work environment thrives on open communication. Think of it as the lifeblood that keeps the organization moving and grooving. When communication lines are open, issues get addressed quickly, ideas flow freely, and everyone feels more connected.

Establishing Communication Channels

So, how do you set up these golden channels of communication? Simple: create multiple avenues for employees to share their thoughts and concerns.

- **Regular Meetings:** Schedule regular one-on-ones, team meetings, and even town halls. These are great opportunities for open dialogue and feedback.
- **Anonymous Feedback:** Not everyone is comfortable speaking up. Anonymous surveys or suggestion boxes can be valuable tools for collecting honest feedback without fear of retaliation.
- **Open-Door Policy:** Encourage an open-door policy where employees feel comfortable approaching their managers or HR with any issues or ideas.

Encouraging Constructive Feedback

Feedback is a two-way street. It's not just about managers giving feedback to employees; it's also about creating a culture where employees feel comfortable giving feedback upwards and sideways.

- **Training on Feedback:** Provide training on how to give and receive feedback constructively. Emphasize the importance of focusing on behaviors, not personalities, and offering solutions along with critiques.

- **Normalize Feedback:** Make feedback a regular part of the workday, not just something that happens during annual reviews. This way, it becomes less intimidating and more of a helpful, ongoing conversation.

- **Recognize and Reward:** Don't just focus on what needs improvement. Recognize and celebrate positive contributions. A simple "Great job!" can go a long way in boosting morale and encouraging a culture of appreciation.

Quote: "Management is about human beings. Its task is to make people capable of joint performance, to make their strengths effective and their weaknesses irrelevant." - **Peter Drucker**, management consultant and author

Conclusion

Creating a healthy work environment is a continuous journey, not a destination. It requires effort, commitment, and a whole lot of empathy. But the rewards are well worth it: higher employee satisfaction, better teamwork, and a more productive and positive workplace overall.

As we wrap up this chapter, remember that a healthy work environment starts with you. Whether you're a manager, an HR professional, or an employee, you have the power to contribute to a positive culture. So, let's take these insights and put them into action. Together, we can build a workplace where everyone feels valued, respected, and empowered to do their best work.

In the next chapter, we'll delve into the importance of early detection and reporting mechanisms for toxic behaviors. We'll discuss how to spot the red flags and what to do when they appear. Ready? Let's continue this journey toward a better workplace!

Chapter 4: Early Detection and Reporting Mechanisms

Hey there! Now that we've laid the groundwork for a healthy work environment, it's time to get into the nitty-gritty of spotting trouble before it blows up into a full-blown crisis. Think of early detection and reporting mechanisms as your workplace's early warning system—a bit like having a smoke detector that alerts you before the flames get out of control. So, grab your magnifying glass and your detective hat. We're about to become workplace sleuths!

The Importance of Early Detection

First things first, why is early detection so important? Imagine you're on a ship, and there's a tiny leak. If you catch it early, you can patch it up before it sinks the whole vessel. The same goes for toxic behavior in the workplace. Catching issues early means you can address them before they escalate and cause serious damage.

Benefits of Early Detection

1. **Minimizing Harm:** Addressing toxic behavior early reduces the emotional and psychological toll on employees. No one likes working in a toxic environment, and early intervention can help maintain a positive atmosphere.

2. **Maintaining Productivity:** Early action prevents disruptions to workflow and keeps projects on track. It's much easier to steer the ship when the seas are calm!

3. **Preserving Team Dynamics:** Tackling issues head-on helps maintain trust and cohesion within

the team. The sooner you address the problem, the less chance it has to spread and affect others.

4. **Protecting the Organization's Reputation:** In the public sector, where transparency and accountability are key, swift action can prevent public scandals and preserve trust in your organization.

Quote: "The true test of a company's culture is how well it treats its people when times are tough." - **Howard Schultz**, former CEO of Starbucks

Reporting Mechanisms

Alright, now that we know why early detection is crucial, let's talk about how to set up effective reporting mechanisms. These are the tools that will help you catch those leaks before they become tsunamis.

Anonymous Reporting Systems

Anonymous reporting systems are like your secret weapon. They allow employees to report issues without fear of retaliation, which is especially important in cases of serious misconduct.

Benefits of Anonymous Reporting:

- **Protection from Retaliation:** Employees can report issues without worrying about backlash, making them more likely to speak up.

- **Encouraging Honesty:** Anonymity allows for more candid reports, giving you a clearer picture of what's really going on.

- **Reaching Broader Issues:** Sometimes, systemic issues only come to light through anonymous reports. These systems can help identify widespread problems that might otherwise go unnoticed.

Implementation Strategies:

- **Online Portals:** Provide a secure online platform where employees can submit reports anonymously. Ensure it's user-friendly and widely accessible.

- **Hotlines:** Set up a confidential hotline staffed by trained professionals who can handle sensitive information.

- **Suggestion Boxes:** For a low-tech option, anonymous suggestion boxes placed around the workplace can also work wonders. Just make sure they're checked regularly!

Regular Performance Reviews

Performance reviews aren't just about evaluating work output; they're a prime opportunity to identify and address potential issues early on.

Key Elements of Effective Performance Reviews:

- **Consistency:** Conduct reviews regularly—quarterly or annually—to monitor progress and address issues promptly.

- **Balanced Feedback:** Offer constructive criticism along with recognition of positive contributions. This balanced approach helps maintain morale while encouraging improvement.

- **Action Plans:** Develop action plans for addressing any identified issues, complete with specific goals, timelines, and support mechanisms.

Quote: "Feedback is the breakfast of champions." - **Ken Blanchard**, author and management expert

Open-Door Policy

An open-door policy is a fantastic way to encourage open communication. It signals to employees that management is approachable and willing to listen.

Benefits of an Open-Door Policy:

- **Accessibility:** Employees feel they can approach decision-makers directly, fostering a sense of inclusion and trust.
- **Timely Resolution:** Issues can be addressed quickly before they escalate.
- **Building Relationships:** Open communication strengthens the bond between employees and management, creating a more cohesive team.

Implementation Strategies:

- **Clear Communication:** Clearly communicate the open-door policy to all employees, emphasizing its purpose and benefits.
- **Manager Training:** Train managers on handling sensitive conversations and providing support.
- **Encouragement:** Regularly encourage employees to use the open-door policy, reinforcing its importance.

Creating a Supportive Environment for Reporting

Even with the best reporting mechanisms in place, they won't be effective if employees don't feel safe and supported in using them. Here's how to create that supportive environment.

Promoting a Culture of Respect

Respect is the cornerstone of a supportive workplace. When employees feel respected, they're more likely to speak up about issues.

Key Strategies:

- **Leadership Commitment:** Leaders must model respectful behavior and hold themselves accountable for creating a positive workplace culture.
- **Inclusivity:** Encourage inclusivity and diversity through policies, training, and daily interactions.
- **Recognition:** Recognize and celebrate respectful behavior, reinforcing its importance.

Training and Education

Knowledge is power. Providing training and education on reporting mechanisms, workplace behavior, and the importance of a respectful culture empowers employees to take action when needed.

Key Training Topics:

- **Identifying Toxic Behavior:** Educate employees on what constitutes toxic behavior and its impact.
- **Reporting Procedures:** Provide clear instructions on how to report issues and the process that follows.
- **Confidentiality and Privacy:** Emphasize the organization's commitment to confidentiality and protecting employees' privacy.

Quote: "Management is doing things right; leadership is doing the right things." - **Peter Drucker**, management consultant and author

Ensuring Confidentiality

Confidentiality is critical in the reporting process. Employees need to trust that their reports will be handled discreetly and professionally.

Key Strategies:

- **Confidential Reporting Channels:** Ensure that all reporting channels protect the identity of the reporting employee.

- **Clear Procedures:** Clearly outline the steps taken after a report is made, emphasizing confidentiality.

- **Sensitive Handling:** Train managers and HR professionals on handling reports sensitively and maintaining confidentiality.

Conclusion

Early detection and effective reporting mechanisms are essential components of a healthy work environment. By implementing anonymous reporting systems, conducting regular performance reviews, and fostering an open-door policy, organizations can encourage employees to report issues without fear. Creating a supportive environment that promotes respect, provides training, and ensures confidentiality further strengthens these mechanisms, making it easier to identify and address toxic behavior.

Next up, we'll dive into the nitty-gritty of addressing toxic behaviors head-on. We'll explore strategies for conducting difficult conversations, setting boundaries, and creating Performance Improvement Plans (PIPs). Ready to roll up your sleeves and tackle these challenges? Let's get to work!

Chapter 5: Addressing Toxic Behaviors

Hey there, workplace warriors! We've covered a lot of ground so far—spotting toxic behaviors, creating a healthy environment, and setting up solid reporting mechanisms. Now, it's time to face the beast head-on: addressing toxic behaviors. Think of this chapter as your ultimate playbook for managing those tricky situations with finesse and empathy. Whether it's having a tough conversation, setting boundaries, or crafting a Performance Improvement Plan (PIP), we've got you covered. So, roll up your sleeves and let's dive in!

Conducting Difficult Conversations

Ah, difficult conversations—the dreaded but necessary part of managing a team. These are the moments when you have to put on your big-kid pants and tackle the tough stuff. It's not easy, but it's crucial for maintaining a healthy workplace. Let's break down how to do this without feeling like you're walking on eggshells.

Preparation

First things first: prep work. A little preparation goes a long way in ensuring the conversation is constructive rather than confrontational.

1. **Gather Information:** Before diving in, make sure you have all the facts. This includes specific examples of the toxic behavior, its impact on the team, and any prior incidents. Facts are your friends in these conversations.
2. **Set Clear Objectives:** Know what you want to achieve. Are you looking to change behavior, clarify

expectations, or simply open a dialogue? Having a clear goal will keep the conversation focused.

3. **Choose the Right Setting:** Privacy is key. Choose a quiet, neutral location where you won't be interrupted. This shows respect for the person and the seriousness of the conversation.

The Conversation

Now, the moment of truth. How do you approach the actual conversation without it turning into a drama fest?

1. **Opening the Discussion:** Start with a clear and calm introduction. For example, "I'd like to discuss a few concerns that have come up regarding your recent interactions with the team." Keep it factual and avoid emotional language.

2. **Providing Specific Examples:** Use concrete examples to illustrate the behavior and its impact. Instead of saying, "You're always negative," try, "During last week's meeting, you interrupted your colleague multiple times, which disrupted the flow of discussion."

3. **Active Listening:** This isn't a monologue. Allow the other person to share their perspective. Listen actively and show empathy, even if you don't agree with everything they say. Sometimes, understanding their point of view can provide valuable insights.

4. **Setting Expectations:** Clearly outline what needs to change and why. For example, "Going forward, I expect you to allow others to speak without interruptions during meetings. This will help maintain a respectful and productive environment."

5. **Concluding the Discussion:** Wrap up by summarizing the key points and outlining the next steps. Express confidence in their ability to make the necessary changes, and thank them for their time.

Quote: "In the end, it's not about who is right or wrong, but about finding a solution." - **Simon Sinek**, author and motivational speaker

Setting Boundaries and Consequences

Once the tough talk is done, it's time to set some ground rules. Think of boundaries as the guardrails that keep everyone on track. They're not just about saying "no"; they're about creating a framework where everyone knows what's expected and what the consequences are for stepping out of line.

Establishing Boundaries

Boundaries help maintain a respectful and efficient work environment. They're like the user manual for workplace interactions.

1. **Define Acceptable Behavior:** Be clear about what behaviors are acceptable and what aren't. This could include anything from communication norms to work ethics. The key is specificity—vague guidelines lead to vague compliance.

2. **Communicate Clearly:** Make sure everyone knows these boundaries. Whether it's through team meetings, emails, or posted guidelines, the message should be loud and clear.

3. **Consistency:** Apply these boundaries consistently across the board. Double standards are a fast track to resentment and confusion.

Implementing Consequences

No one likes to talk about consequences, but they're a necessary part of maintaining order. Think of them as the fine print in your workplace contract.

1. **Progressive Discipline:** Start with a verbal warning and escalate as necessary. For instance, a first offense might warrant a verbal warning, while repeated issues could lead to a written warning, suspension, or even termination.

2. **Transparency:** Be transparent about the consequences for crossing boundaries. Everyone should know the stakes, and there should be no surprises.

3. **Documentation:** Keep detailed records of all incidents and disciplinary actions. This is crucial for accountability and legal protection.

Quote: "Culture is not just one aspect of the game, it is the game." - **Lou Gerstner**, former CEO of IBM

Developing Performance Improvement Plans (PIPs)

Sometimes, despite your best efforts, an employee's performance or behavior doesn't improve. This is where a Performance Improvement Plan (PIP) comes in. Think of a PIP as a structured roadmap to help an employee get back on track.

Key Components of a PIP

1. **Specific Goals:** Clearly outline the specific areas where improvement is needed. Goals should be SMART: Specific, Measurable, Achievable, Relevant, and Time-bound.

2. **Action Plan:** Detail the steps the employee needs to take to meet these goals. This might include

additional training, mentorship, or changes in work habits.

3. **Support and Resources:** Identify the resources available to support the employee. This could be anything from access to training programs to regular check-ins with a mentor.

4. **Timeline:** Establish a timeline for achieving these goals, including regular progress reviews. Make it clear when you'll be checking in and what will be assessed.

5. **Consequences:** Clearly state what will happen if the goals are not met by the end of the PIP period. This could range from further disciplinary action to termination.

Implementing and Monitoring the PIP

1. **Initial Meeting:** Discuss the PIP with the employee, ensuring they understand the expectations and the support available. This should be a collaborative conversation where the employee can ask questions and provide input.

2. **Ongoing Monitoring:** Regularly check in to assess progress and provide feedback. These meetings should be documented and used to track the employee's development.

3. **Final Evaluation:** At the end of the PIP period, conduct a final evaluation to determine whether the employee has met the goals. If they have, acknowledge their efforts and outline the next steps. If not, discuss the potential consequences and next steps.

Quote: "Feedback is the breakfast of champions." - **Ken Blanchard**, author and management expert

Conclusion

Addressing toxic behaviors in the workplace is no easy feat, but it's essential for maintaining a healthy and productive environment. From having tough conversations to setting boundaries and developing PIPs, each step is a vital part of the process. Remember, the goal isn't just to discipline but to guide and support employees toward better behavior and performance.

As we wrap up this chapter, keep in mind that tackling these issues requires a mix of firmness, fairness, and empathy. You're not just managing employees; you're leading them, and sometimes that means making tough calls for the greater good of the team and the organization.

In the next chapter, we'll dive into the legal and ethical considerations of managing toxic employees. We'll explore how to navigate the tricky waters of public employment laws, confidentiality, and ethics. Ready to dig deeper? Let's keep the momentum going!

Chapter 6: Legal and Ethical Considerations

Hey, superstar! You've navigated the tricky terrain of addressing toxic behaviors, and now it's time to explore the legal and ethical landscape. Think of this chapter as your legal GPS, guiding you through the potential pitfalls and ensuring you stay on the right path. Managing toxic employees in public employment isn't just about doing what's best for the team; it's also about adhering to laws and ethical standards. So, buckle up and let's dive into the do's and don'ts of legally and ethically managing toxic behavior.

Understanding Public Employment Laws

First things first: public employment has its own set of rules. Unlike the private sector, public employment involves a higher level of scrutiny and a unique set of legal protections. So, how do you navigate this legal maze? Let's break it down.

Key Legal Protections

1. **Due Process:** In public employment, employees often have a right to due process, especially when facing disciplinary actions. This means they must be given notice of the charges against them and an opportunity to respond. Think of it as their day in court—except, hopefully, less dramatic.

2. **Equal Employment Opportunity (EEO) Laws:** These laws are your best friend when it comes to preventing discrimination. They prohibit discrimination based on race, color, religion, sex, national origin, age, disability, or genetic information. So, when addressing toxic behavior,

ensure that decisions are based on facts and not influenced by these protected characteristics.

3. **Collective Bargaining Agreements (CBAs):** If your organization has a union, you'll likely have a CBA to consider. These agreements outline specific procedures for disciplinary actions and grievances. Always check the CBA to ensure you're following the agreed-upon rules.

4. **Whistleblower Protection:** Public employees are protected under various laws if they report illegal or unethical activities. This is a biggie. Make sure you differentiate between toxic behavior and legitimate whistleblowing. The last thing you want is to retaliate against someone for doing the right thing.

Quote: "The law is the witness and external deposit of our moral life." - **Oliver Wendell Holmes Jr.**, former Associate Justice of the U.S. Supreme Court

Navigating Disciplinary Actions

1. **Documentation:** Keep meticulous records of all incidents, communications, and actions taken. This isn't just about CYA (Cover Your Actions); it's about ensuring a fair and transparent process.

2. **Consistent Application:** Apply policies consistently to all employees, regardless of their position or tenure. Inconsistency can lead to claims of unfair treatment or discrimination, which can land you in hot water.

3. **Legal Counsel:** When in doubt, consult with your legal team. They can provide guidance on navigating complex situations and ensure that all actions comply with relevant laws and regulations.

Confidentiality and Privacy

Next up, confidentiality and privacy. These aren't just buzzwords; they're critical components of managing sensitive situations. When dealing with toxic behavior, you'll likely handle confidential information. How you manage this information can make or break trust within your team.

Confidential Handling of Reports

1. **Confidential Reporting Systems:** Use systems that allow employees to report issues confidentially, protecting their identity and encouraging them to come forward without fear of retaliation.

2. **Limited Disclosure:** Only share sensitive information with those who need to know, such as HR professionals or legal counsel. This helps prevent unnecessary gossip and protects the privacy of all parties involved.

3. **Data Security:** Ensure that all records related to toxic behavior, including reports and investigation notes, are securely stored and accessible only to authorized personnel.

Respecting Employee Privacy

1. **Personal Information:** Avoid disclosing personal information about employees, such as health conditions or family situations, unless it's absolutely necessary for the situation at hand.

2. **Surveillance and Monitoring:** If your organization uses surveillance or monitoring tools, make sure they comply with legal requirements and are clearly communicated to employees. Transparency is key here.

3. **Confidential Conversations:** Conduct all discussions related to toxic behavior in private settings. This not only protects confidentiality but also shows respect for the individuals involved.

Quote: "Privacy is not an option, and it shouldn't be the price we accept for just getting on the Internet." - **Gary Kovacs**, former CEO of Mozilla

Ethical Implications of Disciplinary Actions

Beyond the legal requirements, ethical considerations are crucial. Handling disciplinary actions with integrity and fairness isn't just about avoiding lawsuits; it's about doing the right thing. So, how do we navigate these murky waters?

Fairness and Equity

1. **Impartiality:** Make decisions based on facts, not personal feelings or biases. This is especially important in public employment, where decisions can be scrutinized by the public and the press.

2. **Proportionality:** Ensure that the consequences are proportional to the behavior. For instance, a minor infraction shouldn't result in severe punishment, while serious offenses should be met with appropriate consequences.

3. **Second Chances:** Where appropriate, consider offering employees an opportunity to improve. This could be through additional training or a Performance Improvement Plan (PIP). Remember, the goal is to correct behavior, not just to punish.

Respect and Dignity

1. **Respectful Communication:** Always communicate with respect, even when discussing

serious issues. Avoid using language that could be perceived as accusatory or demeaning.

2. **Support for Affected Employees:** Provide support for employees affected by toxic behavior, whether they're the ones exhibiting it or the ones suffering from it. This could include access to counseling or Employee Assistance Programs (EAPs).

3. **Transparency and Honesty:** Be as transparent as possible about the process, within the bounds of confidentiality. Honest communication builds trust and reinforces the organization's commitment to fairness and integrity.

Quote: "Integrity is doing the right thing, even when no one is watching." - **C.S. Lewis**, author and scholar

Conclusion

Navigating the legal and ethical considerations of managing toxic employees is no small feat, but it's an essential part of maintaining a fair and just workplace. By understanding public employment laws, maintaining confidentiality, and adhering to ethical standards, you can handle these complex situations with confidence and integrity.

As we wrap up this chapter, remember that the goal is not just to manage toxic behavior but to uphold the principles of fairness, respect, and dignity. You're not just following rules; you're setting a standard for what it means to be an ethical and responsible leader.

Next up, we'll explore the different remedial actions and outcomes, from disciplinary measures to termination procedures. We'll also look at how to manage team dynamics after addressing toxic behavior. Ready to dig into the practical side of things? Let's keep this momentum going!

Chapter 7: Remedial Actions and Outcomes

Welcome back, workplace champions! You've navigated the tricky waters of identifying toxic behaviors, set up effective reporting systems, and tackled the legal and ethical considerations. Now, it's time to roll up our sleeves and dive into the nitty-gritty of remedial actions and outcomes. Think of this chapter as your toolkit for managing the aftermath of toxic behavior—from disciplinary measures to termination and everything in between. We'll also explore how to support the team after the storm has passed, ensuring a smooth transition back to normalcy. Ready? Let's do this!

Progressive Discipline

Progressive discipline is a structured approach to addressing misconduct or underperformance. It's all about giving employees a fair chance to improve while maintaining a safe and productive work environment. Think of it as a step-by-step process, where each step escalates only if the previous ones don't resolve the issue.

Steps in Progressive Discipline

1. **Verbal Warning:** The first step is usually a verbal warning. This is an informal conversation where you address the behavior, explain why it's problematic, and set expectations for change. It's not about pointing fingers; it's about having a candid discussion to nip the problem in the bud.

2. **Written Warning:** If the behavior continues, it's time for a formal written warning. This document outlines the specific issues, previous verbal warnings, and the consequences of continued

misconduct. It serves as an official record and underscores the seriousness of the situation.

3. **Suspension:** For more severe or repeated offenses, a suspension (with or without pay) might be appropriate. This gives the employee time to reflect on their behavior and its impact on the workplace.

4. **Final Warning:** This is the last stop before termination. A final warning clearly states that any further violations will result in dismissal. It's the employee's last chance to turn things around.

5. **Termination:** If all else fails and the toxic behavior persists, termination may be the necessary and final step. This decision should never be taken lightly and must be backed by thorough documentation and adherence to legal protocols.

Quote: "The culture of an organization is its most important asset." - **Brian Chesky**, CEO of Airbnb

Grounds for Termination

Termination is a significant action with far-reaching consequences, both for the employee and the organization. It's crucial to ensure that any decision to terminate is fair, justified, and well-documented. Let's explore some common grounds for termination.

1. **Gross Misconduct:** This includes actions like theft, violence, harassment, or severe insubordination. Such behavior warrants immediate dismissal due to its severe impact on the workplace.

2. **Chronic Underperformance:** Consistently failing to meet performance standards, despite ample opportunities for improvement, can be

grounds for termination. It's not just about numbers; it's about the effort and willingness to improve.

3. **Violation of Policies:** Breaching critical company policies, such as confidentiality agreements or safety protocols, can justify termination. These rules exist for a reason, and violating them can put the entire organization at risk.

4. **Legal or Ethical Violations:** Engaging in illegal activities or actions that severely breach the organization's ethical standards can lead to immediate termination. In public employment, these breaches can also damage public trust.

Termination Procedures

1. **Investigation:** Before terminating an employee, conduct a thorough investigation to gather all relevant facts and evidence. This step is crucial for ensuring a fair and informed decision.

2. **Documentation:** Document all incidents, communications, and actions taken. This not only supports the decision but also provides legal protection if the termination is challenged.

3. **Final Meeting:** During the termination meeting, communicate the decision clearly and respectfully. Explain the reasons for termination, refer to documented incidents, and outline any final steps, such as severance packages or the return of company property.

4. **Exit Process:** Ensure that the exit process is handled smoothly and professionally. This includes revoking access to company systems, collecting

company property, and providing information about final pay and benefits.

Quote: "In the end, it's not about who is right or wrong, but about finding a solution." - **Simon Sinek**, author and motivational speaker

Managing Team Dynamics Post-Toxicity

Once the immediate issue of toxic behavior has been addressed, it's time to turn your attention to the rest of the team. The departure of a toxic employee can leave a void, create uncertainty, or even disrupt the harmony within the team. So, how do you manage the aftermath and ensure a smooth transition?

Rebuilding Trust and Morale

1. **Open Communication:** Hold a team meeting to address the situation openly and honestly, while respecting confidentiality. Acknowledge the impact of the toxic behavior and the actions taken to resolve it. This transparency helps rebuild trust and shows that management is committed to maintaining a healthy work environment.

2. **Support and Counseling:** Offer support services, such as counseling or Employee Assistance Programs (EAPs), to help employees process their emotions and any lingering stress. Remember, it's not just about the person who left; it's about the team members who stayed behind.

3. **Recognition and Appreciation:** Acknowledge the resilience and hard work of the remaining team members during a challenging period. Recognizing their efforts can boost morale and reinforce a positive work environment.

Re-establishing Norms and Expectations

1. **Reinforce Policies:** Revisit workplace policies and behavioral expectations with the team. This is a good opportunity to clarify any ambiguities and emphasize the importance of maintaining a respectful and collaborative workplace.
2. **Encourage Feedback:** Create an open forum for employees to share their thoughts and concerns. This feedback can provide valuable insights into how the team is feeling and any areas that may need attention.
3. **Foster Inclusivity:** Promote inclusivity and diversity within the team. Encourage team-building activities that help strengthen relationships and create a sense of belonging.

Quote: "The true test of a company's culture is how well it treats its people when times are tough." - **Howard Schultz**, former CEO of Starbucks

Implementing Long-Term Solutions

Addressing the immediate effects of toxic behavior is only half the battle. To prevent future issues, it's essential to implement long-term strategies that foster a positive and inclusive workplace culture.

Continuous Monitoring and Improvement

1. **Regular Assessments:** Conduct regular assessments of workplace culture and employee satisfaction. Surveys, focus groups, and one-on-one interviews can provide valuable insights into how things are going and where improvements can be made.
2. **Leadership Training:** Invest in leadership training to equip managers with the skills they need to recognize and address toxic behavior effectively.

Strong leadership is key to maintaining a positive workplace culture.

3. **Policy Updates:** Regularly review and update workplace policies to ensure they remain relevant and effective. This includes updating protocols for reporting and addressing toxic behavior.

Encouraging a Positive Culture

1. **Celebrate Successes:** Regularly celebrate team and individual successes. Recognizing achievements fosters a positive atmosphere and encourages continued excellence.

2. **Promote Work-Life Balance:** Encourage a healthy work-life balance by offering flexible work arrangements and supporting employees' well-being.

3. **Nurture Employee Development:** Provide opportunities for professional development and growth. A culture that values learning and development can enhance job satisfaction and reduce the likelihood of toxic behavior.

Quote: "Integrity is doing the right thing, even when no one is watching." - **C.S. Lewis**, author and scholar

Conclusion

Managing the aftermath of toxic behavior is a delicate process that requires careful planning and thoughtful execution. From progressive discipline to termination and team recovery, each step is crucial for maintaining a healthy and productive work environment. Remember, the goal is not just to address the behavior but to create a lasting positive culture that supports and values all employees.

As we wrap up this chapter, keep in mind that the journey toward a positive workplace culture is ongoing. It requires continuous effort, open communication, and a commitment to doing what's right—even when it's hard. You're not just managing a team; you're shaping the future of your organization.

In the final chapter, we'll delve into real-world case studies and practical examples, showcasing how other organizations have successfully handled toxic behaviors. These stories will provide valuable lessons and inspiration as you continue your journey toward a healthier workplace. Ready to learn from the best? Let's get inspired!

Chapter 8: Case Studies and Practical Examples

Hey there, rockstars! We've journeyed through the highs and lows of managing toxic employees, from spotting the signs to implementing solutions and everything in between. Now, it's time to get into some real-world stories—those "been there, done that" moments that bring theory to life. In this chapter, we're diving into a treasure trove of case studies and practical examples. These stories will show you how other organizations have navigated the tricky waters of toxic behavior, turning potential disasters into valuable lessons. So, grab a comfy seat and let's get inspired!

Case Study 1: The Passive-Aggressive Saboteur

Background:
In a state health department, an employee named Mark was a classic passive-aggressive saboteur. Mark had a habit of subtly undermining colleagues, whether by withholding information, spreading half-truths, or "forgetting" to complete critical tasks. This behavior caused friction within the team and disrupted workflow.

Challenges:

- **Identifying the Behavior:** Mark's actions were subtle and often flew under the radar, making it difficult to pinpoint the issue.

- **Team Dynamics:** His behavior created an atmosphere of mistrust and frustration, leading to low morale and high stress levels among team members.

Approach:
The department's HR team conducted a series of

confidential one-on-one interviews with the team to gather more information. Once the pattern of passive-aggressive behavior was confirmed, Mark's manager had a candid conversation with him, using specific examples of his actions and their impact. Mark was put on a Performance Improvement Plan (PIP), with clear expectations and regular check-ins.

Outcome:
Mark initially resisted, but the clear documentation and consistent feedback helped him realize the seriousness of the situation. Over time, he made noticeable improvements in his communication and collaboration skills. The team gradually rebuilt trust, and overall morale improved. The department also implemented regular team-building activities to foster a more supportive environment.

Key Takeaways:

- Subtle toxic behaviors require careful observation and thorough documentation.
- A PIP can be an effective tool for encouraging behavioral changes.
- Team-building activities can help repair and strengthen team dynamics.

Quote: "You can't change what you don't acknowledge." - **Dr. Phil**, psychologist and TV host

Case Study 2: The Chronic Complainer

Background:
In a county public works department, an employee named Susan was known for her constant complaints. From the workload to the temperature in the office, Susan found fault with everything. Her negative attitude was contagious, affecting her coworkers' morale and productivity.

Challenges:

- **Distinguishing Between Valid and Invalid Complaints:** While some of Susan's concerns were legitimate, her approach was overwhelmingly negative, making it difficult for her manager to address the issues constructively.
- **Team Morale:** Susan's constant griping created a toxic atmosphere, leading to decreased motivation and engagement among her colleagues.

Approach:
Susan's manager decided to address the situation head-on. In a private meeting, they acknowledged the valid points Susan raised but emphasized the importance of constructive feedback. Susan was encouraged to use the department's anonymous suggestion box for her concerns and to offer solutions along with her criticisms. The department also started a weekly "team check-in" to discuss any concerns openly and constructively.

Outcome:
With an outlet for her concerns and a platform to discuss them constructively, Susan's attitude began to shift. She started participating more positively in team discussions and even suggested a few practical improvements. The overall atmosphere in the office improved, and the team became more cohesive and solution-oriented.

Key Takeaways:

- Distinguishing between valid concerns and toxic negativity is crucial.
- Providing constructive outlets for complaints can turn a negative situation into a positive one.
- Open forums for discussing issues can help prevent negativity from festering.

Quote: "Complaining is not a strategy. The best leaders can offer solutions." - **Jeff Bezos**, CEO of Amazon

Case Study 3: The Overly Assertive Manager

Background:
In a city planning office, a new manager, Jessica, was overly assertive in her approach. While her intentions were to drive results, her methods came off as abrasive and dictatorial. Jessica often dismissed her team's input, made unilateral decisions, and criticized staff publicly.

Challenges:

- **Communication Style:** Jessica's management style created a culture of fear and resentment, stifling creativity and collaboration.
- **Employee Retention:** Several employees considered leaving due to the hostile work environment, raising concerns about turnover.

Approach:
The HR department conducted an anonymous survey to gauge employee satisfaction and identify the root causes of discontent. The feedback highlighted Jessica's leadership style as a significant issue. The HR team then facilitated a coaching program for Jessica, focusing on emotional intelligence, active listening, and collaborative decision-making. Additionally, a new protocol was introduced for decision-making processes, requiring team input and consensus.

Outcome:
Jessica gradually adjusted her approach, becoming more open to feedback and inclusive in her decision-making. The coaching sessions helped her develop better interpersonal skills, and she began to build stronger relationships with her team. Employee satisfaction improved, and the office atmosphere became more collaborative and supportive.

Key Takeaways:

- Leadership style can significantly impact workplace culture and employee morale.
- Coaching and training can be effective tools for developing better management skills.
- Inclusive decision-making fosters a more engaged and motivated team.

Quote: "The function of leadership is to produce more leaders, not more followers." - **Ralph Nader**, political activist and author

Case Study 4: The Disruptive Innovation Advocate

Background:
In a public transportation agency, an employee named Alex was passionate about innovation. However, his enthusiasm often came across as disruptive. Alex frequently criticized existing systems, ignored practical constraints, and pushed for unrealistic changes, creating tension within the team.

Challenges:

- **Balancing Innovation and Practicality:** Alex's push for innovation clashed with the agency's established procedures and budget limitations.
- **Team Dynamics:** His dismissive attitude toward colleagues' ideas led to friction and decreased collaboration.

Approach:
The agency's leadership recognized the value of Alex's innovative ideas but needed to channel his energy constructively. They established an innovation task force, including Alex and other team members, to explore new projects within realistic parameters. Clear guidelines were

set, including budget constraints and collaborative processes.

Outcome:
The task force successfully implemented several pilot projects, balancing innovation with practical considerations. Alex learned to value teamwork and became more receptive to feedback. The agency benefited from fresh ideas, and the team dynamic improved, fostering a more inclusive and supportive environment.

Key Takeaways:

- Channeling disruptive energy into structured innovation can harness its potential.
- Clear guidelines and collaborative frameworks help balance innovation and practicality.
- Encouraging teamwork and inclusivity can turn a potential disruptor into a valuable contributor.

Quote: "Innovation distinguishes between a leader and a follower." - **Steve Jobs**, co-founder of Apple Inc.

Conclusion

These case studies offer a glimpse into the real-world challenges and successes of managing toxic behaviors in public employment. They illustrate that, while toxic behavior can present significant obstacles, it also provides an opportunity for growth and improvement. The key is to approach each situation with a blend of empathy, fairness, and a commitment to the well-being of the entire team.

As we wrap up this chapter, remember that every workplace is unique, and there's no one-size-fits-all solution. However, by learning from these examples, you can gain valuable insights and strategies that can be adapted to your specific context. You're now armed with a comprehensive understanding of how to navigate the complexities of toxic behavior and create a healthier, more productive work environment.

Quote: "The culture of any organization is shaped by the worst behavior the leader is willing to tolerate." - **Gruenter and Whitaker**, organizational consultants

With these real-world insights and the knowledge from previous chapters, you're well-equipped to tackle toxic behaviors in your workplace. The journey toward a positive work environment is ongoing, but with the right tools and mindset, you can lead your team to success. Here's to a brighter, healthier, and more collaborative future!

Conclusion: The Road to a Thriving Workplace

And there you have it! You've navigated the twists and turns of handling toxic employees in public employment, armed with strategies, real-world examples, and a deep understanding of the complexities involved. From identifying the first signs of toxicity to implementing long-term solutions, you've been on a journey toward creating a healthier, happier workplace. So, let's take a moment to reflect on what we've learned and where we go from here.

The Power of Proactive Management

Throughout this book, we've emphasized the importance of being proactive rather than reactive. Waiting until a situation reaches a boiling point only makes it harder to manage. By setting clear expectations, establishing robust reporting mechanisms, and addressing issues head-on, you're not just putting out fires; you're preventing them from starting in the first place.

Proactive management isn't just about avoiding problems; it's about creating an environment where everyone can thrive. It's about setting the stage for collaboration, respect, and innovation. Remember, a positive workplace culture doesn't happen by accident—it's built with intention and care.

Quote: "An ounce of prevention is worth a pound of cure." **- Benjamin Franklin**

The Human Element

At the heart of every workplace are the people. Whether you're a manager, an HR professional, or a team member, it's essential to remember that we're all human. We all have our strengths, weaknesses, and unique perspectives.

Approaching situations with empathy and understanding can make all the difference. It's not just about enforcing rules; it's about nurturing growth and fostering a sense of community.

In dealing with toxic behavior, empathy doesn't mean excusing harmful actions. It means understanding the root causes and working towards a constructive solution. Whether through coaching, providing resources, or, when necessary, making tough decisions like termination, the goal is always the same: to protect the well-being of the team and the organization.

Quote: "To handle yourself, use your head; to handle others, use your heart." - **Eleanor Roosevelt**

Embracing Continuous Improvement

Creating a positive workplace culture is not a one-time effort but an ongoing commitment. It requires regular reflection, feedback, and adaptation. The workplace landscape is ever-changing, with new challenges and opportunities constantly emerging. By fostering a culture of continuous improvement, you encourage innovation, resilience, and a shared sense of purpose.

Encourage open communication, seek feedback, and be willing to evolve. Celebrate successes, learn from setbacks, and always strive for a better tomorrow. The work you put in today will pay off in a more engaged, motivated, and cohesive team.

Quote: "The only way to do great work is to love what you do." - **Steve Jobs**

The Journey Ahead

As you close this book and step back into your day-to-day responsibilities, remember that you're not just a manager or an employee; you're a steward of your organization's culture. You have the power to shape the environment in which you and your colleagues work. By applying the principles and strategies you've learned, you can make a lasting impact that goes beyond resolving conflicts or managing difficult situations.

The journey toward a thriving workplace is filled with challenges, but it's also incredibly rewarding. Every positive change, no matter how small, contributes to a larger, more vibrant work environment. So, take pride in your role, stay committed to your values, and continue to lead with integrity and compassion.

Quote: "The future belongs to those who believe in the beauty of their dreams." - **Eleanor Roosevelt**

Final Thoughts

Thank you for taking this journey with us. We hope this book has provided you with valuable insights, practical tools, and a renewed sense of purpose. As you move forward, keep these lessons close to your heart and continue striving for a workplace where everyone feels valued, respected, and empowered.

Here's to creating a work environment that not only excels in its mission but also enriches the lives of everyone involved. You've got this, and we can't wait to see the incredible things you'll accomplish. Now, go forth and build the positive, dynamic, and thriving workplace of your dreams!

Quote: "Be the change that you wish to see in the world." - **Mahatma Gandhi**

Thank you for being a part of this journey. The road ahead is bright, and we're cheering you on every step of the way. Let's make the workplace a better place for everyone, one step at a time.

Further Resources

Navigating the complexities of handling toxic employees and fostering a positive workplace culture can be challenging. For those looking to deepen their understanding and find additional support, here's a list of valuable resources, including books, websites, professional organizations, and tools. These resources offer a wealth of knowledge and practical advice to help you continue your journey toward a thriving work environment.

Books

1. **"Crucial Conversations: Tools for Talking When Stakes Are High" by Kerry Patterson, Joseph Grenny, Ron McMillan, and Al Switzler**
   - A comprehensive guide to handling difficult conversations with clarity and confidence.

2. **"The Five Dysfunctions of a Team: A Leadership Fable" by Patrick Lencioni**
   - This book explores the common pitfalls that can hinder team dynamics and offers practical strategies for overcoming them.

3. **"Dare to Lead: Brave Work. Tough Conversations. Whole Hearts." by Brené Brown**
   - A must-read on courageous leadership, vulnerability, and building trust within teams.

4. **"Radical Candor: Be a Kick-Ass Boss Without Losing Your Humanity" by Kim Scott**

- This book provides a framework for giving honest feedback while maintaining empathy and respect.

5. **"Emotional Intelligence: Why It Can Matter More Than IQ" by Daniel Goleman**
   - An insightful exploration of emotional intelligence and its critical role in personal and professional success.

Websites and Online Resources

1. **Society for Human Resource Management (SHRM)**
   - www.shrm.org
   - A leading resource for HR professionals, offering articles, research, and tools on various workplace topics, including managing toxic employees.

2. **Harvard Business Review (HBR)**
   - www.hbr.org
   - An excellent source for articles and case studies on leadership, management, and organizational culture.

3. **MindTools**
   - www.mindtools.com
   - Provides practical resources for personal and professional development, including guides on conflict resolution and communication.

4. **LinkedIn Learning**
   - www.linkedin.com/learning

- Offers a wide range of online courses on leadership, management, communication, and emotional intelligence.

Professional Organizations

1. **American Management Association (AMA)**
   - www.amanet.org
   - Offers training and resources on management and leadership development.

2. **International Association for Conflict Management (IACM)**
   - www.iacm-conflict.org
   - A professional association that promotes the understanding and resolution of conflict through research and education.

3. **The Conference Board**
   - www.conference-board.org
   - A global, independent business membership and research association providing knowledge and tools for effective organizational management.

Tools and Assessments

1. **DiSC Personality Assessment**
   - A popular tool for understanding individual behaviors and improving workplace communication and teamwork.

2. **Myers-Briggs Type Indicator (MBTI)**
   - A well-known personality assessment that helps individuals understand their

personality types and how they interact with others.

3. **Gallup StrengthsFinder**
   - An assessment tool that helps individuals identify their strengths and leverage them in the workplace.

4. **Employee Assistance Programs (EAPs)**
   - Many organizations offer EAPs that provide confidential counseling and support services to employees facing personal or professional challenges.

Online Communities and Forums

1. **HR.com**
   - www.hr.com
   - A community platform for HR professionals to connect, share insights, and access resources.

2. **Reddit - r/AskHR**
   - www.reddit.com/r/AskHR
   - An online community where users can ask questions and share advice on HR-related topics.

3. **Quora**
   - www.quora.com
   - A question-and-answer platform where professionals share expertise on a wide range of topics, including workplace management and conflict resolution.

Podcasts

1. **"WorkLife with Adam Grant"**
   - A podcast that explores how to improve the way we work, featuring insights from top leaders and experts.

2. **"Dare to Lead" with Brené Brown**
   - Discussions on courageous leadership, vulnerability, and building trust in the workplace.

3. **"The Look & Sound of Leadership" with Tom Henschel**
   - Offers practical tips on leadership and communication, helping professionals develop their skills and enhance their impact.

These resources offer a wealth of knowledge and practical advice, providing additional support as you navigate the complexities of managing toxic behaviors and fostering a positive workplace culture. Whether you're looking for in-depth books, online courses, or professional networks, these tools can help you continue your journey toward a thriving work environment.

www.ingramcontent.com/pod-product-compliance
Lightning Source LLC
Chambersburg PA
CBHW071958210526
45479CB00003B/991